73

Black Abacus

CႽ

poems by Ian Keteku

Write Bloody North

writebloodynorth.ca

First edition.
ISBN: 978-0992024529

Cover Design by Katrina Noble
Interior Layout by Winona León
Edited by Alessandra Naccarato
Proofread by Keaton Maddox
Author Photo by Jason Hennessy

Type set in Bergamo from www.theleagueofmoveabletype.com

Write Bloody North
Toronto, ON

Support Independent Presses
writebloodynorth.ca

*For my grandmothers
and their mothers*

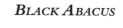

BLACK ABACUS

BLACK ABACUS

A Delicate Skeleton

Moment One 15
Thursdays 16
Bookmark 17
Point of Boiling 18
Arrival One 19
Crocodile Skin 20
The Night Is Always Awake 22
Season Three 23
Lesson One 25
Intermission 26
This House We Built Downwards 27
The Prophet 32

Thief

Thief One 37
Adam 38
Black Prayer 39
Prince Aladdin—Terrorist One 40
Missing God 43
Are You a Muslim? 44
Thief Two / Hibernation 45
Are You a Practicing Muslim? 46
Thief Three / Birthday 47

Eulogies in Brail

How to Kill a Poet 51
The Amazonian Guard 54
Tonight's Prayer Is for Him 55
Borders 56
Gallery One, Alabaster 57
Season One 58
Natasha. Natasha. Natasha 59

Braille 60
Ransom 61
Paradise 62
A Million to One 63
Goliath 64
Perspective 65
Season Four 66
Take Care 67
Things I Have Caught 68
Fourteenth Round 69
The Night Trump Won 70
Five Photographs, One Flash 72
Things Which Have Caught Me 73
Sacrifice One 74

Burning is Becoming

Forgiveness 79
Elephants 80
David 81
Mutima 82
Monarch 83
Anansi the Spider Searches for Love 84
Kepler's Third Law 86
Quantum Leap (e=nhv) 87
Eschatos One 89
Eschatos Two 90
Abacus 91

A Delicate Skeleton

∴ a martyr before I was born

MOMENT ONE

I remember my birth
like it was tomorrow, the unholy sensation
of abandon, accepted struggle,

my mother's womb a burning revolution,
promise on fire.

I do not recall the choice to be burning,
wayward archeologist
searching for sky in uncharted ground.

Before my skin, colour of handcuffs
became fodder and fuel
for a war I was born into,

clock hands pointing towards a verdict,
seat-belt light off
crash landing into tomorrow.

Mother bled a lament
we could both see tomorrow,

I arrived a blessing fragmented,
a dark-skinned schism.
My cry so familiar, it was heard in the past.

THURSDAYS

My head is wood on a wooden desk.
Class begins and I am already
a dense mess of shavings:

today's the day, I've decided.

The teacher and I
have a relationship to mortar, this hour
we are both softer
than the silence between us.

Seeing the decision in my eyes
she sends me to the office,
where the counselor asks questions,
treats me like kindle.

They both figure the reason
I want out of this life
is because my parents ~~discipline~~ beat me.

For sixteen weeks, a case worker
watches our family be a family;

a studio audience in our living room,
staining the loveseat awkward
searching for splinters, a missed line,
peeling bark.

Every Thursday, our Father displays
rare parts, affectionate
and palm leaf, a steady Capricorn carrying
an almost suicide on his back.

After the case worker leaves,
we stay on stage,
play our parts perfectly.
Hit all the lines for a few more hours
until Friday morning shrivels us back
to who we truly are.

BOOKMARK

a soft *yes*
serenading clifftop, pensive Appalachian
and Himalayan hurt
and an empty Bible sitting restless and fearful

and once I checked out the story of my life
and returned it the next day
I couldn't relate to the protagonist
he was too "not enough"
I will wait for the sequel—it reminds me
of autumn;
how beautiful must it all be—before it all
dies again.

I believe in something
I am too young to love,
and I am afraid
I am too old to know
when it arrives.

POINT OF BOILING

Charred and taunting its privilege,
what temperature do memories burn?

Ash has stained our trembling teeth,
our mouths reluctant of water.

Are memories best served warm?

On a silver tongue, dripping river Delta,
slave ships and servitude

in this loud burning,
our faces singing ballads of the blaze.

Our histories, completed in napalm
remember the roots, the scars,
the smell, Icarus' dream
and the smoldering truth

that a fire cannot be quenched
with oil, with blood.

ARRIVAL ONE
January 1979

My mother's first month abroad,
she's welcomed to Missouri with winter.
Her classes end late, too late
to study the sun.

In the darkness she holds a dilemma:
approach the German Sheppard
conveniently let loose, or walk through
the graveyard and risk being bitten
by something much sharper than teeth.

My mother was raised on hot soup and myth;
both kept her alive this far.
She knows ghosts need a voice to see,
holds her breath tightly

past tombs, sprints the last stretch,
collapses her chest, and watches
her fear form to fog.

The German family with the German dog
rent her a frozen den.
She keeps on her jacket, closes her eyes
and smells hot-pepper soup.

CROCODILE SKIN

most juvenile crocodiles
are born with obituaries

unknowingly
trot in shallow waters
proud and inquisitive
along dangerous terrain
never knowing the foreshadow of their existence

never grow into emperor
kings of marsh and salt-water
hold wisdom and flesh
in the caverns of their teeth

most
will not see adulthood
because the distinct colour of their skin
makes them targets for predators

makes them targets for predators
because the distinct colour of their skin
will not see adulthood
most

in the caverns of their teeth
hold wisdom and flesh
kings of marsh and salt-water
never grow into emperor

never knowing the foreshadow of their existence
along dangerous terrain
proud and inquisitive
trot in shallow waters

unknowingly
are born with obituaries

THE NIGHT IS ALWAYS AWAKE

We nick name her darkness, obsidian.

Only ghosts are alive
in the dead of the night, we say.
Granted we are scared
and when we are scared

we become everything but gracious.

We accuse the darkness
of the myths we made up about her
and night falls into melancholia
knowing it is not the abyss of black
our eyes claim it to be.

The sun was not her first-born child.
She holds so much more light inside her,
offers constellations as conciliation.

How much slander must she drink
before she can start breathing again?

She is always awake.
Not nocturnal, she hangs still,
a warm compromise,
smoke in a windless room.

This is how it goes for dark things.

To be both hazard-sign and hospitable,
feared and necessary.

The night gets nightmares
every time she thinks of herself.

Season Three

I.

My summer chore for most summers is cutting the grass.
Front yard, back.

Our lawn mower looks like a rabid mastiff, caged in gas
and thirsty to cut.
Once the machine finally commits to the biting, push it slow,
the kind of soft found at the altar.

When it is done, it is done. You are proud:
you gave something to a home that it couldn't give to you.

You can smell the grassy aroma best in the evening, right before
twilight, can taste it.
The damp air holding sweetness in suspension.

The smell of fresh cut grass always makes the work worth it.
The scent, both blue collar and calligraphy. A forest of photographs.
Green blue-jean stains. The shaky tumble
through youth, insect bites.
How something so small can break through the toughest of skin,
a reminder of how soft we truly are.

II.

The smell, right before twilight, a distress signal.
Silent song, a cry from one blade to another, a warning—
you could be next, sharpen your edges, stand firm in your roots.
They cannot cut all of us. At least not all at once.

They will call you unruly. Say you are too free too wild and abundant
on this avenue, pile your bodies in trash, ready for compost.
Say the death of one feeds the rest of them.
Like your murder was necessary, something to make the house look pretty,
keep up the neighbourhood.

Like death is reparation for growing too much. Like the other side is greener.
The smell of our fresh cuts and open wounds; incense for the séance.
Like it doesn't hurt every time.

And neighbours watch in silence. They hear the devastation.
They smell the killing, right before twilight.
Your flesh desperate for the season to change. Look sharp.

One day the old lawn mower caught fire.
I thought, this is perfect. Finally, the castle collapses.

LESSON ONE

Every Ghanaian child has tasted
the thin of a cane, branches of a whip,
the teeth of a belt, parent's hands calloused
from years of delivering proverb.

We are taught to be lily pad.
Full, floating and weary of waver,
lest we drift
into the unknown night.

Taught to be polite and hard-broiled,
cordial with flame, respect law
like the rule of physics.

If you fall, you will hit
the ground arrested, in jail
or dead.

We are taught there is poison
beyond the pulp, the shell
of an avocado pit, and trouble will find
black men like smoke
finds a place to surrender.

Lesson one: the burden of bearing
something black, give thanks

for training beneath the bruises,
mistakes honoured with wooden spoons,
the voice that has made us tender,

soft enough to ignore
the gnawing burden
of being born a black lily pad
in the middle of a windstorm.

INTERMISSION

Father's fist

and my mother's face

sometimes sang duet

never on pitch

one always louder than the other

I blamed myself

for not being able to compose

an intermission to this

symphony of stitches

THIS HOUSE WE BUILT DOWNWARDS

Our first home
lives inside me. A memory of sunlight, soot. Muted laundromat—
spinning foreshadow, washing secrets to no avail. There exists
only one photo of me in that home, resting defenceless
in my mother's hands. This photo, proof: the home did exist.
I existed within it, too young to know it to be true.

Our second home,
I can still smell. Ice cream cones and prairie soil. A desolate
worm, a kingly reward. I learned to be more brother than bother,
rap battles   wrestling matches
broken vases   broken dishes
broken noses   broken trust
it was not the first home   my father broke
with secrets.

Then, our home
touched the Atlantic, covered by omnipotent sun and shade
on skin. Our pedigree resting in a gazebo of artifacts. I began
to decode the language I had only known through arguments
and laughter. My father's secrets grew lazy, rustic, exhausted.
It became apparent he was no longer willing to wear
a clandestine cloak.

We moved
into our last home carrying new furniture: cashmere couch,
chandelier, fetish mask. The old skeletons found their ways
into bed sheets and pantries, laundry baskets and bookshelves.
Our last home was our last home together. Hidden in the
suburbs, with a view of the Rockies, eroding with the pace
of our gospel. Nuzzled on stolen burial ground, I wonder
what the graveyard thought of the dying family living inside.
The house was huge, an immigrant's mansion: sauna in the basement,
backyard full of fauna. The walls smelled of voodoo, money
and forged smiles. This house took the place of our teeth.

When it finally broke, our home
fractured, a trillion magenta maggots
feeding off the idea
of what could have been.

THE PROPHET

There is a used bookstore on Kingston Road,
a block away from the lake,
where the sand is shallow,
where I bought *The Prophet*, five dollars, no tax.

On the first page, an inscription in cursive,
sharp and round like a swimmer's dance.

> *Ian… because you are so special for me…*
> *Love, Doris.*
>
> *February 14, 1981*

★

In this story Doris is from Sarajevo.
She writes, *you are so special for me*,
English an unbuttoned shirt on her tongue.

When the forests began whispering of war,
her family bet on a horse
in the shape of a town and fled

to Savannah, Georgia, where Doris
begins sweeping the floor
of the peeling Orthodox church,
caressing dust off the organ,
replacing melted candles with holier ones.

Every Saturday, matinees are half price
at the drive-in, where Ian cleans the projector
for three dollars an hour, saving to buy
his uncle's red Chevrolet.

This is where they meet. I imagine
their love is a call to morning
at dusk, and at dusk, amber soaking in song.

★

Valentine's day, 1981.
At the city's edge, Ian's red car
is a robin overlooking the last willow in the valley.

Doris smiles
and hands him a book.

★

In this story, they do not last.
War sends some away, it beckons others back.

Ian keeps the book in the attic,
in the same box as the films
he stole from the drive in.

When he dies, his daughter Almitra
donates the book.

★

For thousands of days,
The Prophet travels across the continent,
through deserving hands, as prophets do.
The Prophet waits by the beach
as prophets do.

Almitra asks the prophet
to tell her about love and the prophet says,

> *Love has no other desire, than to fulfill itself.*

A book with my name, written in cursive.
A prophecy fulfilling itself.

THIEF
...and other vocations

THIEF ONE

Three men hung like mist
along a crucifix judgment.

Two were thieves,
one the self-proclaimed son of God.

As their bodies dripped justice
into bygone-bark,
benediction burned.

One of the men became legacy
for everything here and after here.
His life story, love story
written in chapters
of the world's most notorious text.

The other two, a footnote.

We may never know their names,
just that they were thieves

just that they died
just that they died next to him.

ADAM

He named man Adam, meaning dust.

He named man Atom, a unit of matter.

Man named himself matter, Atom.

Man made himself matter, Atom Bomb.

Man made matter into dust, Adam into Adam.

Ameen, Ameen, Ameen.

BLACK PRAYER

Dear Lord,

the dark enters quickly,
a sabotage in the stomach of a broken twilight.
My life a whisper
with no ear to call home.

I am a ghost in the shape of a man,
balancing between the history of my hide
and the glow of my future.

Today I survive the silence;
tomorrow I will let the shadows escape
and paint my crimes
on the canvas of catastrophe.

PRINCE ALADDIN—TERRORIST ONE

I.

as-salāmu 'alaykum
peace be upon you

A boy older than the internet
or young enough to be hurt by it
is granted three wishes.

> *bismillah*
> *as-salāmu 'alaykum*
> peace be upon you

Words spit sloppy on mirror,
his face a propane tank,
the arson of a world
mispronouncing his name:

Street rat. Sand nigger. Camel jockey. Terrorist.

Peace. and quiet. his first wish.
But silence is golden, so he steals
only what he can't afford

and that's everything.

II.

Some wishes only last
the length of a shooting star.
He looks for escape,
for solace in sideways,
in over and under,
in dynamite prayers.

On his back, a monkey
dressed as a joke, an afterthought.
A reason for war.

There is a jihad brewing in his throat.
He coughs, the second wish
falls out helpless, kisses his cheek.

The magic in transformation,
in becoming the stolen prophecy of others.

III.

His last wish,
to stop wishing for wishes

and write his legacy
as a billow of blue smoke.

MISSING GOD

The night I lost the god I was born with, a silver song sat
on my bed, smiling proud. It dressed in a cold hymn, dishonest
and metallic, a spoon after the last lick of gelato.

Jesus left a note on my headboard saying, *be back in five minutes.*

I waited. Couldn't find him; not without an address,
birth certificate, social security number.
Most gods are frauds, others are on social assistance.

I searched. Through mathematics and Christmas cards,
my mother's reassurance. Through my pastor's footsteps
and the church's stained tea cups.

The night white Jesus forgot to return, other deities
entered the room. Each singing miracles of forgiveness, offering
their best sales pitch. I glazed my tongue along the buffet of holy:
half-crescent moons, wickers and wicks, a singing brass bowl.

Choosing a new god is an exercise in surrender:
putting trust in the unknown, risking my faith
on someone who might not believe in people like me.

Are You a Muslim?

They ask
with frost-bitten judgment
dangling off each syllable.
A winterized inquisition:

Are   you   a   Muslim?

My answer
a wedding-day wolf
dressed in the husk of a little girl.

I try not to reply too proud,
over zealous.
Avoid their icicle eyes
crowning me threat.
The nickname I give to God
mutes my achievements,
exposes shrapnel treaties beneath my teeth.
I try not to reply too meek,
too lampshade liberal,
not Godly enough for fanatics.

The game of God is a tight-wire walk
along fire without blistering, without falling
and still seem nervous
though your soul sinks in sediment.

I eventually reply,

I   am   Muslim   … ish

and whisper grace
before considering the next sip of spirits.

Thief Two / Hibernation

As winter approaches—easy,
undisciplined and necessary—

animals of all traditions gather
and forage, hoard and collate
amulets to nourish themselves in cold times.

And as winter approaches, she is leaving.
So we gather and forage, hoard and collate

our phones with all the memories
we can hold, with all the time
we have left.

We find these moments
in undisciplined places,
in the unlikely and unpredictable.

We hold them in the safest of spaces
like rations, like last resorts.
Nourishment until the skies again
start speaking in sun.

Are You a Practicing Muslim?

Practice—

like religion is a skateboard,
Eighty-eight keys, sex.
Like the more you do it
the better you'll be.

In truth,
I practice Islam like I practice piano:
once a day, when falling
behind,

when the sky is more blue than usual,
when love migrates south.

I go to the mosque when times get tough,
the night before an exam,
hoping prophets have empathy
for the uninspired.

Allah is gracious, merciful and patient.
So I give thanks to the indigo skyline,
to this slowly unrusting faith.

Lord knows working with me
takes a whole lot of practice.

THIEF THREE / BIRTHDAY

Some of my friends start planning their birthdays
a day after their last one, remembering

a joyful panorama,
black celebration, smiling.

But every year someone is absent;
sick with the flu, sick with the news,
tired from chasing themselves into grey.

Someone had babies,
another couldn't handle the smog
and those friends who will never return.

We pray it is not a heavy sick,
the lottery of cancer, plain old time.

We pray it is not the police;
for their mother's sake,
for the sake of the next time,
and the next time, and this time.

We pray it is not one of us;
someone else's family
someone else's friend.

We call out their names,
like a name carries a gun,
like our complexion carries the threat.

We are angry, sad and bewildered.
We pray for their mothers,
sick of the news.

We change the subject
until it is the only thing we are talking about
until all the cake is gone.

EULOGIES IN BRAIL

+closed mouths
saying everything
we thought
we already knew

How to Kill a Poet

I.

Don't start with one.

An intelligent morning,
first day of kindergarten, cold hearts,
promises to prophets, the morning's puncture, dry brush in fresh ink.
One is the only number signifying a beginning;
it is not the way to kill the poet.

Start with zero.

0.

Tell him this is the number
of people his words meant anything to: two.

I.

Do not use numbers in your attempt.

Start with scalpel,
cut tongue from heart. Staple his gums
to page twelve. At the bottom,
right by the foot.
Note how low self-esteem rises

from his jealous marrow.

Open your browser,
show them profiles of his cousins,
distant high school friends, their spouses
and their little thems,
and their mountains of stuff.

Dreams are for people without enough stuff.

Commandeer from the top shelf
a poetry book about nature. Written by an older, whiter poet
with awards, with stuff.
Melt the ISBN number; give it to him to drink.

I.

What is the difference between God and a poet?

God doesn't think they're a poet.

I.

Don't tell the poet it's a joke.

He will laugh,
but his insides will be all cocaine cavalier,
Stanford prison experiment.
He'll swallow the guilt of his stigmata, his stuff.

Open a new tab. Go on YouTube, play a video of a baby in Syria
or one with malaria in Nigeria, zika in Venezuela.
Recite his oppression back to him, auction off his most expensive lines.

Place your finest synagogue socks
in his left hand, show him how wool is both beautiful and useful,

and his poems have no way to keep us warm.

I.

Fill his deadlines with his dead lines, burn all his books,
don't leave any prints.
Place a stick of dynamite in amnesia,
the poet will disintegrate wholly.

See him break
into melancholy, lose himself in the madness,
no one to dance with at the search party.

Force him to write his own eulogy,
but do not let him sign his name:

no one needs to know he is gone.

I.

Be cautious and careful

when trying to kill a poet.
You are likely to become the poem itself.

THE AMAZONIAN GUARD

What happens when your purpose
is dragged through the sand,
a bullet to its memory?

Gifted death in gratitude,
breast-fed martyrdom, never learning
how to love without force,
without holy chain-mail thunder
dancing through rumor.

What happens when forever ends
before you are ready—

how do you react
when your revolution dies
barely dressed, golden gun spilling
on camera?

TONIGHT'S PRAYER IS FOR HIM

His eyes a screaming masjid.
The splintered violin in his throat
cannot be called crying;

it is incantation,
it is supplication to a God

whose existence is in contention.

He holds
the ruins of Damascus,
twins.
One boy, one girl clutching
them earnest

as though their souls were still there.

BORDERS

As children
we are taught to colour with the lines,
direct our hands within thick
black borders.

We learn something is wrong
if our fingers play nomads,
illegal immigrants outside the borders.

Our dreams were never meant
to be box-cutter highways, censored skylines,
redrawn with someone else's voice.

Our bodies
composed of miracle and light
protest against the borders
of our skin.

We are larger
than the appendix strapped
to the spine of your heart.

Flood the streets with gallons
of you, let them taste the iron
of your life's graffiti,
like a swirling car crash
staining their teeth.

Gallery One, Alabaster

I once sat in fear so long
I became it, it felt like home

if home were pin prick,
a dim flame
in the mouth of a waterfall.

You cannot eat fear,
sell or trade it for anything warm.

I do not run when I see it, anymore.
I know it is there; I try to be still,
restless and hungry in the gallery
of the alabaster dream.

Season One

Winter is a racist season.
Callous screeches chalkboard against African pelts,
forcing us to lather our melanated bodies with white cream.

Tis the season of white religion, white snow
a pseudonym for debilitating the ghetto.
White Santa with a God complex, gifting decent children
with capitalism's finest novelties,

punishing others with charcoal offerings,
the colour of us.

Natasha. Natasha. Natasha

It worked for Candyman, for Beetlejuice.
But not all ghosts reanimate
when we speak in repetition,
bribed with sobbing, with handmade memorials
dancing to wailing heart beats. Natasha,

perhaps the drink we drank in your honour
wasn't strong enough; the liquor we poured,
not enough spirit; too much concrete kiss,
not enough magic. Natasha.

Natasha, a woman at the grocery store stole your face
pressing for bruises on plums.
I think of the bullet your stomach ate   by accident
I think of your name, a refrain with no song,

Subhan'allah.

BRAILLE

When you are surrounded by darkness,
you begin to see in the dark

and embrace the beauty in pollution,
colour in shadow.

Ransom

I'd rather be taken for ransom
than for granted.

When stuck in the solitude of another,
hope has an expiration date.

And begins the barbed-wire embrace,
the powder-keg kiss I convinced

myself to love, arctic burning
the back of my guilt.

I call the devil by name,
offer begonias dipped in sunlight;

I negotiate my bail
with promises I am too weak to keep.

PARADISE

Paradise is not buried
beneath the blueprint of honey.

It is tossing uncertainty,
hurling wet pearls
against arrogant foundations

until fingers bleed a metaphor:
shattered snake eyes,

the elusive tail of paradise
curling around the corner
you just left searching.

A MILLION TO ONE

Pyramids cannot be moved by hands,
or the tongue's iron offering.
Some walls soften only with time,
and failing tyranny.

Still we hunt for peace in lands
forged from suffering,
seek love from people still learning its ropes.

We chase the likely impossible in unlikely places:
underneath the sneer of a shadow,
ballot boxes, the Alamo.

Behind a cubicle desk, unintentionally collecting
impossibles, gentle reminders on half-violent parchment.

And so it goes with impossible things:
when the mirage is close enough to touch,

the dream opens its eyes.

GOLIATH

They will say
your great quest is too colossal
to be conquered with pebbles,

that destiny is found within a boardroom
of rotting aspirations.

For those burning bridges, brandishing
knives intended for spines:

learn where to put your trust,
who to give your heart.

Just because you fell and no one caught you,
doesn't mean they don't love you,

It means the Earth
will always have your back.

PERSPECTIVE

Without direction
a river bullied by horizon

becomes ocean,
a cup of water to a fly.

You have not learned
the lesson of the dirt
until you can drown in a teardrop;

shallow is relative,
deep a vague comparison.

Sorrow is more at home
in a smile and with eyes closed,

blood is not red
but an ocean coated in onyx.

Season Four

I take the path leaving town,
end up in the forest. Realize when a tree
falls in love you can hear it in your bones,
nursing secrets as old-school as instinct.

The wind commits murder against the sky;
it is as loud as lightning, laughter.

I believe the leaves are chasing me,
conspiring with my shadow to file for divorce.

The backs of my hands claim
I don't know them anymore,
my skin organizes a coup. These trees,
heaven's toothpicks, notice the matchbox

in my pockets, the chimney in my chest,
brimstone body-bag hanging from my fingers.

Past the carnage of thorns,
mouthful of ash, my pockets ablaze.

The woods tell me
there is a difference between
       acting out of love
       and acting when out of love.

       It is time to take the path back home.

Take Care

Take care of the great hunger, a bone basket
parading our inadequate hearts.

Take hold of all you decided to break,
and unbreak in your arms, a brittle bullet,
a beautiful sin.

Take precaution in gavel-like laughter,
the court jester's sabbatical.

He sinks in sand, a mirror towards the rapture
embraces the horror,

calls it professional development,
calls it self-care.

Take care, for no map has ever protested
only one way to reach the peak.

THINGS I HAVE CAUGHT

1. Her eye: once, never again. Not like that first time.
2. Malaria.
3. A handful of screams.
4. Wind of the fact the wind cannot be caught.
5. What I thought was the holy spirit; it was just the flu.
6. An old flame, still burning, just not for me.
7. A dead lightening bug.
   Are dead lightening bugs still lightening bugs?
8. My breath after her smile told me the truth.
9. A prayer from heaven.
10. Myself catching myself, again.

FOURTEENTH ROUND
for Azuma Nelson

You can ask about me
        the most notorious coward
in this party of puzzles.

I was once a nice guy
until they took my kind eyes
for *weak knees*

and besides,

this life is twelve rounds surviving
looking to be a little less forgiving, less butterfly-sting.

In that corner there will be blood,
a canopy of whistles holding something permanent.

In this corner
the end of the road, I will be there, busted and bruised,
a lonely boy to mend.

When forced to choose
between already   and becoming

just remember:
When the fight is stronger than fear, when the title
is worth defending, when giving up means calamity,

only then can I say that I've won.

THE NIGHT TRUMP WON

The wind,
wrestles a restless brick face,
challenges it to a yelling match.

The hearts,
insomnia addicts,
pray half-heartedly
to a melancholy sky.

    I find comfort in a voice
as far as prophecy,
there is a heavy in her tremble—

no amount
of devastation, impending barbiturate bellow,
will soften the strength
of her promise:

      wars will conjure
      bodies, will break
      the sky, sad for some time to come.

And even though my skin
and her modest heart attract
misfortune, we take stock,

count all the blessings left.

The tides have changed the wind,
more abrasive,
everything around seems uncertain.

      Except this moment,
      her unwavering voice
      a mountain, steady in the belly of chaos,

a reminder:
despite the fear falling from shadows,
dripping from weeping horizons,

there is always her voice.

FIVE PHOTOGRAPHS, ONE FLASH

Huron

When she places her lips on my ear,

I listen the way silk listens to skin,
pavement to rain, canvas to muse.

Erie

I place my ear on her chest. A steady rumble—serene
congestion. A timid giant tugging
at something it has not yet learned to hold.

Superior

She places her ear on my chest.
Yesterday's photograph, still developing. Still negative.
Blots of colour, crawling edges.

Michigan

I listen to her belly,
the dream of another heartbeat. Small yet prophetic.

He does not have my eyes;
        I listen until he does.

Ontario

In her hand is a gift. Small yet prophetic. Husk pastel
and kaleidoscope. I found it on the beach.
I hear the ocean, crashing hush, water on water on wind.

*It is not the ocean you hear, but the sound of blood
flowing past your ear.*

All blood journeys through vessels.
Maroon waves, an uncertain tomorrow at my ear.

THINGS WHICH HAVE CAUGHT ME

1. Her eye.
2. Myself, red handed, a layer of sacrifice glistening from the pores.
3. Her embrace, by surprise, stuck and sticky in a web of lies.
4. Myself catching myself again.

SACRIFICE ONE

Satan's love for God
was so terribly mammoth he would rather flood himself in fire
than share his father's affection with another, let alone a human.
What is the devil but a broken heart falling from heaven?
And so it goes, that Cain killed Abel—he thought God loved
his brother more, and Jesus loved Judas and Judas loved jewels
and God so loved the world he allowed Judas to betray Jesus
with a kiss on the cheek.

And he bled,
cardinal sacrifice. Fountains of forgiveness spilling from his wrists.
Scarlet roses melting onto crucifix. What is Christ but a broken heart
heading towards heaven? And so it goes. The ones you love will hurt
you the most.

I imagine Romeo
finding his beloved beyond breath. Body stone-still like an amethyst
photograph. Or Juliet, to die and resurrect only to find the love
you came back for fading like a memory in the hands of a ghost.
Such incredible hurt. Such miraculous melancholy. And so it goes.

BURNING IS BECOMING

∞ a benediction

FORGIVENESS

The aged birch

holds within its belly of bark
a dogma of forgiveness.

Even the lumberjack
hell-bent on bending its branches
into slices of tables and paper
to soak the mud of poets,

the birch forgives.

Alloy waters, bellyful
of metallic regret
feed our insecurities, nourish our egos
as we continue to confuse its blue
with items we no longer love,

still the water forgives.

The mountain range near where I was born
has kissed the wind's sharp
for so long its skin speaks in stone.

It does not admonish the wind's embrace,
thankful for the language which made it tall.

Allah, give me the mood
of the birch, the river's personality.

My apologies run dry
in the damp doorway of pain.

Lend me their strength
so my pardons are true—timeless, luminescent—

that I may one day be broken open,
wide and avalanching.

ELEPHANTS

Elephants do not pray for water,
do not ask the sodden clouds
what they know of mercy,
expect baptism in return.

The elephant has faith.
Somewhere there is water,
will trudge through miles of suffering
and storm just to find it.

Most promises are glow sticks
illuminating everything once broken.

We can pray for mercy;
we must also walk towards it,
follow thirst until the migration breaks us,
until we are embossed
with embarrassment, dusty and damp
for the first time, again.

Inshallah, we will get there
as long as there is beauty
in our breathing.
Nothing is immune to the softness of stone,

in the next room
a thirsty elephant almost drowning.

DAVID

When life is a bird's nest
in the courtyard of a breeze,
when sorrow sits squinting
at your gaze,

dress your love in riot gear
and grow the last drop of your beauty.
Hold it to the light,
blossoming in your hands.

As you dip toes
onto the shoreline of mercy,
know you are both sand and acropolis,
mercy and retaliation.

When you grow tired of shoveling
someone else's darkness,
when you finally negotiate
a pair of retired wings,

dance amongst the cinder smudges
of blue whiskey midnight.
Know you are dream and dreamer,
caretaker and the mess,

an inadequate banquet,
a calm handshake,

and your fingers Goliath's regret.

Mutima

Give me your hand I will show you forever,
open your palm and I will read you a love story.

When God burnt melancholy in the skies
and traced envy in dirt,
molded our ancestors from mud, scissored
our thoughts into thoughts,
God forgot, or so we thought, to give us a heart.

Then came the day when our maker had to leave,
rest from slitting wrists to breed glaciers,
retire the holy shotgun, shooting stars to birth planets
    then pause.

But before God set forth, the Alpha and Omega
left us with a heart no larger than a fist, a reminder of her.

The heart was left weeping, screaming across the Serengeti,
the Red Sea middling its way into the Mediterranean
and stopping in the Nile.

    How could our mother leave us, asked the heart.

Sun, moon, darkness and rain had no answer. After eons
of mourning, after three forevers and two days, the crying heart
carefully carved a home in the chest of man.

    Said the heart, *There is no absolute synonym*
                 for love except God.

    Give me your hand, I will show you forever
    open your palm and I will read you a love story.

from Uganda, of a heart named Mutima
waiting for the love of its life to return home.

MONARCH

Two doors down lives a woman
with more years behind than ahead,
tough as tenderness, soft as retribution.

She finds a prayer in her garden, shrubs
and convictions blend themselves within each other.
During the profanity of winter, plants pretend to be whispers,
only alive if you choose to listen, choose to imagine.

By spring's benediction, they garnish the sidewalk green
looking like weeds, resembling nuisance.
When July finally steams in, flowers sing of freedom,
loud and afflicted.

Her garden is more than a garden;
it is a dirty party trick,
the most alluring insignia
amongst this arcade of characters.

She longs for human connection
and her plants—the bait, I am snared by a rose.

The poet in me searches for metaphor,
clawing its way out of this tiny forest
watching a dying someone loving something into life.

ANANSI THE SPIDER SEARCHES FOR LOVE

After a life of spinning,
it is time to quilt a home
in the shape of someone else.

His neighbours, the giraffes,
have been together for years;
their long spotted necks
hold each other like a pocket of prayer beads.

Anansi insists the giraffes come see
the ballad he built in the blue jays' nest.
The couple peek their heads
through the branches of an old tree,
heads bending to the sway of the song,
necks twisting against each other
as they sweep amongst the above.

Anansi spins a web around them,
weaves in and out of their limbs,
long and resting
until the two lovers are twined
and spotted in silk.

He waits for love to appear,
a day, a week, millions of moons,
hoping to trap it in his web.

A world's worth of midnights,
as the grandchildren of the jays turn grey,

until he is an old spider
and his arms can no longer spin,
shriveled and rippled from waiting.

He would ask
why love has not yet come
but Mr. and Mrs. Giraffe are dust and bone,
waltzing lofty in the after-world.

Love cannot be lured
by a beautiful song in the nest of orphans
or trapped by the cobwebbed legs of a trickster.

KEPLER'S THIRD LAW

Have you heard the music on the moon?
—
Jupiter off key, God with a trench coat
conducting the stars.

Does it sound like home,
remind you of love?

The harder you look, the louder it gets,
I promise.

If you cannot hear the music,
dissonance is in your heart,
if this choir of unfolding
neglects to put rivers in your eyes,

it is because you have forgotten
that you are the music,

a song inspired by revolutions
around the sun, the anthem of angels
if angels were anthems.

Encore.

QUANTUM LEAP (E=NHV)

Backs on the water, eyes on Orion,
the cosmos move with candor

We push Olympic breaths
into the sky

and the sky whispers back
a secret.

★

There will be a moment,
a moment in the history of us,
where the rules of Einstein
and Newton and Nietzsche
crumble like clocks in a tsunami.

Maybe our bones will be dust
before we get a chance to witness
a complete transcendental transformation,
a metaphysical revolution.

But at that moment, I will walk
through you, become a part of you,

a bed of daffodils,
cloud of playground laughter,
the stars in a sequin dress.

★

The sky stops breathing.

I count six meteors
from inhale to exhale.
With each blazing conclusion,
wish for another
as bright as ever,
more Olympic than the last

and finally hear our hearts flutter
like a hummingbird in a tsunami.

ESCHATOS ONE

Nyankopon nnkum wo a, odasanyi ku wo a, innwu.

If the Supreme Being has not killed you
your destiny is not yet due.

—Akan Proverb

We are the portraits of our decisions,
a chorus of bad choices.
Somewhere the saints have given up
and god is trapped in the whiskey's empty.

It is time to bid adieu, say goodnight to it all,

kiss its nickel-covered eyelids,
rosemary for remembrance,
and hope for redemption.

It is libation to the skies, a eulogy for extinction,
one last chance to make love to the moon.

One final bow, denouement
in a night gown. A palm of books
and the book of psalms,
a candle buried by the darkness.

The final moment is quiet,
burning lullabies on your skin. It is proud,
screaming whispers into your ears.

Tonight, say goodbye to the all souls
waiting a lifetime to become music.

Eschatos Two

We are yoctometers of neutrino zeptometer,
long quarks protons neutrons nuclei in love

at gamma ray wavelengths, grains of sand
singling falsetto, hail and brain storms.

We are oak trees and 747s, the Vatican,
Everest insomnia and Pluto, Medusa, Islam

Sagittarius, messiah
and Berlin, and poetry, and Einstein.

We've married our nightmares,
had affairs with our dreams:

memories trapped in the grey hairs
of our ancestors, the broken hearted

brontosaurus, polar bears born
into melting homes.

We are light years of fortune,
a history of hurt, a prophecy of joy,

a couplet on a page
in the most magnificent of fables.

ABACUS

I have heard the secret of the abacus
and now I count ethereal things.

I am half the man I need to be,
an arrow with two left feet,
stomach space for just
five more tragedies.

I have too many of my father's hands.

★

Truth is an imaginary number
the square root of faith, an average of lies.
Once, a man made a meat from my poison,
this too a sign of war.

Three cheers
for the lesser of two evils,
the crow with the righteous heart.

I count riches and the rainy days
and look for the radius of love.

★

The difference between
a memory and a dream
depends on which one you'd rather follow:
both irrational, impossible to prove.

I count two starlets, one moonstone,
each time a bloom whispers her indivisible name.

What number of miracles can you count on
before the abacus turns back?

NOTES

"The Amazonian Guard" is a group of women bodyguards employed to protect former Libyan leader Muammar al-Gaddafi.

"Azuma Nelson" is a Ghanaian retired boxer. He has held the WBC featherweight title and twice the WBC super featherweight title.

"Mutima" is the Swahili word for "heart." The poem is based on an Ugandan creation myth.

"Anansi the Spider" is a character in many Ghanaian folk tales.

"Kepler's Third Law" states, the square of the orbital period of a planet is directly proportional to the cute of the semi-major axis of its orbit. His three laws provided insight to the motion of planets around the sun.

"e=nhv" is also known as Planck's Formula. It helps describe the energy of a photon.

"Eschastos," originally Greek, refers to "the last," can also be used to describe the "last days."

ACKNOWLEDGMENTS

To the takers of risks, the dreamers and everything
they dream about, to the mentors, the mentees, the
poets, the preachers, the imams, the Uber drivers
and their families, to the editors and the publishers,
to the orators and the slammers, the storytellers,
bass players, the recipe, my brothers, my sisters (in
blood and in love), the afrofuturist painter, the famous ones,
and those still waiting to break, community,
the mc's, the emoticon, the teachers, the learners,
the ancestors and their ancestors

to you, who offered your everything
when I only asked for your ear.

Give thanks.

About the Author

IAN KETEKU is an award-winning poet and multi-media artist, the 2009 Canadian national slam champion and the 2010 World Poetry Slam champion. Born and raised by Ghanaian parents, his work is strongly influenced by his upbringing and journeys throughout Africa. A devout practitioner of Afrofuturism—a philosophy of projecting the black experience into a celestial, technological future—he was featured in the CBC documentary, *IF the Poet*, and he has collaborated with the governments of Denmark, Morocco and Ghana, the Bill and Melinda Gates Foundation and may others.

Ian has produced two albums and acclaimed short-films, and conducts poetry, writing and performance workshops nationally and internationally. *Black Abacus* is his debut collection.

www.ianketeku.com

WRITEBLOODY NORTH
QUALITY CANADIAN BOOKS

Write Bloody North publishes groundbreaking voices and legends of spoken word to create innovative, fresh poetry books.

We believe that poetry can change the world for the better. We are an independent press dedicated to quality literature and book design. We are grassroots, DIY, bootstrap believers. Pull up a good book and join the family. Support independent authors, artists, and presses.

Want to know more about Write Bloody North books, authors, and events? Join our mailing list at

www.writebloodynorth.ca

CPSIA information can be obtained
at www.ICGtesting.com
Printed in the USA
LVHW012141020719
623040LV00001B/59